Great Gorilla Grins

Great Gorilla Grins

An Abundance of Animal Alliterations

by
Beth Hilgartner

Illustrated by
Leslie Morrill

Little, Brown and Company
BOSTON   TORONTO

ILLUSTRATIONS COPYRIGHT © 1979 BY LESLIE MORRILL

TEXT COPYRIGHT © 1979 BY BETH HILGARTNER

ALL RIGHTS RESERVED. NO PART OF THIS BOOK MAY BE REPRODUCED IN ANY FORM OR BY ANY ELECTRONIC OR MECHANICAL MEANS INCLUDING INFORMATION STORAGE AND RETRIEVAL SYSTEMS WITHOUT PERMISSION IN WRITING FROM THE PUBLISHER, EXCEPT BY A REVIEWER WHO MAY QUOTE BRIEF PASSAGES IN A REVIEW.

FIRST EDITION

Library of Congress Cataloging in Publication Data

Hilgartner, Beth.
   Great gorilla grins.

   SUMMARY: A collection of alliterative descriptions of a variety of animals.
   1. Vocabulary—Juvenile literature. 2. Alliteration—Juvenile literature. [1. Alliteration. 2. Animals—Fiction] I. Morrill, Leslie H. II. Title.
PE1449.H5   428'.1   78-10364
ISBN 0-316-36235-2

Published simultaneously in Canada
by Little, Brown & Company (Canada) Limited

PRINTED IN THE UNITED STATES OF AMERICA

for my mother
happy birthday!

LION

Large, lordly lion lounges
limply on a limb.
Lazy Lord Lion leaves Lady Lioness to
land lunch and lovingly launder
little lions.

DUCKS

Dripping and dabbling in dingy, dark water,
ducks dispense with daintiness.
No dandified ducks — too damp!
Ducks desire drizzly days.

RACCOON

Ring-tailed raccoon, though ravenous,
first rinses his repast.
Though he raids without rancor,
he rouses rage.
Unrepenting, rascally
robbing raccoon retreats—
And later repeats.

PONIES

Whether peaceful in pastures or pertly prancing,
pretty ponies please people
by pulling pony-traps, or
patiently permitting patting.

PUSS

Padding primly, puss patrols the parlor.
She perches, purring, on plump pillows, peering and preening.
Prowling among pantry platters, puss pilfers protein from her people's plates.

PENGUINS

Prim penguins parade and pose
in perfect pomp,
puffed up with pride and importance.

SEALS

Silky, shining, sleek seals love
sliding on slick, slippery slides
into icy seas.
Seal-schools instruct small seals to stay
shyly out of sight, since seals'
skin is so scrumptiously soft.

KOALA

Carefully cuddling her cub,
koala cleverly climbs eucalyptuses,
to escape cruel carnivores.

PORCUPINE

A pincushion on paws plods, without poise,
through pinecones.
A paragon of pacifism, the porcupine
can painfully prod pugnacious predators.

GORILLA

Great gorilla grins,
a grimace of grinders.

SNAKES

Shimmery, scaly, and slender, snakes slither stealthily, or sunbathe on stones. Seemingly smirking, snakes slyly set serpentine snares. Snagging scamperers, they squeeze squirming supper to swallowable stillness.

MOLE

Mole mercilessly mines meadows, making mounds to mark his murky, muddy mansion.
Mole's mining methods manage to madden Man.

CAMELS

Camels act contentious, cantankerous, and combative,
if crossed;
But consistent concerned care can create cooperation
conducive to capable, competent conveying
of cargo and kings.

PEACOCK

Peacock inspects and prunes his plumes until perfectly pleased and poised. Proudly, he parades his primped perfection for the poor, plain peahen to peruse and approve.

FOX

For a feast of fowl,
famished fox fights fearlessly,
furtively fooling furious farmers.
He feasts, then flies to freedom.

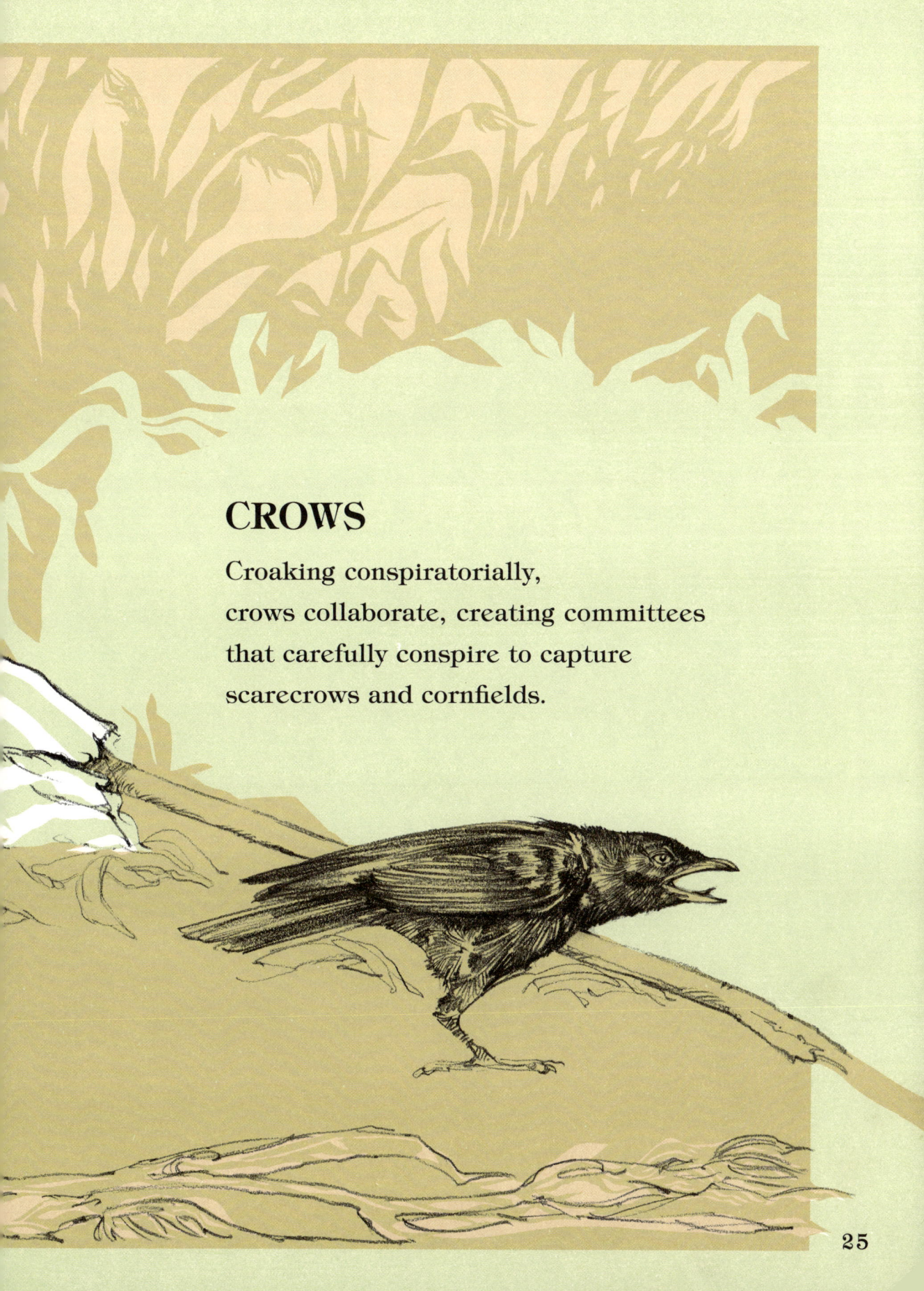

CROWS

Croaking conspiratorially,
crows collaborate, creating committees
that carefully conspire to capture
scarecrows and cornfields.

HARES

Hares hide in healthy hedgerows
or hop happily,
hunting heavenly herbs.

HOUNDS

Hounds hunt hares.

BABY BEARS

Bumbling and benign, baby bears barge through blueberry bushes.
They bang and bash backpackers' belongings while backpackers climb birches.
Beware!
Bigger bears are nearby!

PIGLETS

Plentiful, portly porkers poke
in piles of potato peelings.
Piggies play peacefully in puddles.
Poor plump piglets!
People appreciate pork pies.